The Descent of God

The Ancient Message
Exodus 19, 20

Jeffrey D. Johnson

Wipf & Stock
PUBLISHERS
Eugene, Oregon

Wipf and Stock Publishers
199 W 8th Ave, Suite 3
Eugene, OR 97401

The Descent of God
The Ancient Message: Exodus 19, 20
By Johnson, Jeffrey D.

ISBN 13: 978-1-55635-078-8
ISBN 10: 1-55635-078-3
Publication date 11/30/2006

About Israel Today Ministries

Three-fold Purpose:

- Teach the Church about Israel
- Teach Israel about their Messiah
- Help feed those in need (Romans 15:27; Genesis 12:1-3)

To receive Dr. Johnson's "teaching letters," or, if you would like to send a gift to Israel Today Ministries, or if you would like Dr. Johnson to speak at your church event, school, or small group, contact:

Israel Today Ministries
P.O. Box 150288
Arlington, TX 76015
Phone/Fax 817.468.4441
E mail: Galileeman@juno.com

This is Yossef (Joseph) and Abigail. Your monthly donations help feed little ones like these.

"Inasmuch as ye have done it unto one of the least of these my brethren, ye have done it unto me" –Jesus, Matthew 25:40

About Dr. Jeffrey D. Johnson

- Three decades in ministry
- Founder/Director of Israel Today Ministries
- Director of tours to the Middle East
- Senior pastor in Ohio, Massachusetts and California
- Almost 7 years directorship with International Ministries to Israel (formerly, The American Association for Jewish Evangelism, where the famed Hyman Appelman was the first president)
- Conference speaker
- Bible expositor
- Guest lecturer
- Author

Born and raised in the Midwest, Dr. Johnson took his B.D. from Massillon Baptist College, his MA from Moody Bible Institute, and his Th.M. and Th.D. from Christian Bible College. His passion for Israel, the Jewish roots of Christianity and Bible prophecy, is well known. His teaching will stir your heart to follow the Lord and to love and *"pray for the peace of Jerusalem"* (Psalm 122:6).

As an "Itinerant Bible Teacher," Dr. Johnson will travel anywhere to proclaim God's redeeming Grace through our Lord and Savior Jesus the Messiah, *"to the Jew first, and also to the Greek"* (Romans 1:16).

His call is to *"Teach the Church about Israel; Teach Israel about their Messiah; and to feed those in need"* (Genesis 12:3; Romans 15:27).

Dr. Jeff and his wife, Louise, have purposed to serve the Lord trusting God to provide the funds and resources for their livelihood.

Israel Today Ministries, founded by Dr. Johnson, is a faith ministry, supported by "love offerings" from those desiring to bless Israel. Dr. Jeff and Louise have been commissioned and sent out by their home church.

Comments from Christian Leaders

I am pleased to recommend him to churches as an able expositor of the Word of God.

– *the late* **John Walvoord**, Chancellor,
Dallas Theological Seminary

A Bible Expositor with special insights on the origin, nature and destiny of God's chosen people, Israel.

– **John C. Whitcomb**, Bible Scholar, Author, Professor

A careful expositor of Scripture.

– **Homer Kent**, President Emeritus,
Grace College and Seminary

A practitioner of all that he preaches.

– **Paige Patterson**, former President of the
Southern Baptist Convention, President,
Southeastern Baptist Theological Seminary

He has a wonderful grasp of Jewish history and liturgy.

– **Edgar C. James**, Professor, Moody Bible Institute

He is a person who has been uniquely prepared by God to preach and teach about God's special people. Any one who hears him will come away with a great love for the people of Abraham.

–**Dick Dahlquist**, Chair, Pastoral Studies, Acting Dean,
Grace College of Graduate Studies

He has a gifted teaching ministry which encompasses Biblical prophecy and insights into modern-day Judaism.

–the late **Paul Tassell**, Bible Scholar, Author,
former National Representative of the G.A.R.B.C.

He has a great ministry.

– **LaVerne Butler**, former President of Mid-Continent Baptist College, Scholar, Conference Speaker, President, Pulpit Aflame

Your heart will be thrilled as he ministers the prophetic Scriptures.

– the late **Alden A. Gannett**, President Emeritus of Southeastern Bible College, Bible Scholar, Author, Conference Speaker, President, Gannett Ministries

He loves the people and nation of Israel. He has given himself to a thorough study of God's ancient people and of the prophetic.

– **Ivan H. French**, Pastor Emeritus, Pleasant View Bible Church, former Professor, Grace College and Seminary

The Ancient Message

In Exodus 19 we have the account of Moses' encounter with God and the receiving of the Torah (Pentateuch, or the first five books of the Bible). It has been almost 2,000 years since God communicated with man in such a direct fashion. The first time was with Adam. Now Moses is chosen to hear, and he will write down, the words of God.

What a responsibility, what a fearful thing to stand before a Holy God!

The Revelation of God

One year before, Moses, keeping the flock of Jethro his father-in-law, led the herd to the backside of the desert, and came to Mount Sinai. There he saw a bush on fire, and yet it was not consumed. He carefully approached the bush with great curiosity.

A marvelous thing happened. God spoke to Moses from the midst of the bush (Exodus 3:4). God told Moses not to come near until he took off his shoes, for he was standing on "holy ground." The Lord told Moses to go back to Egypt and to lead His chosen people, the Jews, out of Egypt and thus out of bondage. God said to Moses, "When thou hast brought forth the people out of Egypt, ye shall serve God upon this mountain" (Exodus 3:12).

Moses went down to Egypt and confronted the Pharaoh. Moses, along with Aaron, "went in and told Pharaoh, Thus saith the Lord God of Israel, Let my people go." The confrontation with Pharaoh, which included the ten plagues and the Passover unfold within a year's timeframe.

Moses leads the people out and pass through the Red Sea and experience the miracle of God's provision and protection. Now Moses and the tribes of Israel, free from the enslavement and chains of Pharaoh, knowing that God provides and protects, camp before the Holy Mountain of God.

The Ascent

"And Moses went up unto God" (Exodus 19:3)

How good it was for Moses to go up the Mountain. How good it is for man to ascend the mountain of God. It takes courage. It takes commitment, it takes faith, and you must go alone.

"The Lord called unto him out of the mountain"

David writes, "Blessed is the man whom thou choosest, and causest to approach unto thee, that he may dwell in thy courts: we shall be satisfied with the goodness of thy house…" (Psalm 65:4)

When you approach God in faith, He will call to you. When you struggle on the rocky cliffs of life's experiences and you look up to the Father of Lights, He will comfort and give you instruction.

"And Moses went up unto God" – As the psalmist wrote, "He bowed the heavens also, and came down…He rode upon a cherub, and did fly: yea, he did fly upon the wings of the wind" (Psalm 18:9,10).

Moses ascended and as the cloud covered the mountain, as the fire and lighting appeared (vss. 9,16,17,18), and with the thunder, the earth began to quake and the mountain shook. It is said by the ancients, that as the mount quaked, it began to ascend up to God as the Almighty descended upon this lowly planet.

As Moses went up to God, he did not know whether to approach the cloud, to embrace the cloud, or to stand still and bow before God's presence.

The people in the camp trembled (vs. 16) and Moses cried out to God and God answered him (vs. 19) "And the Lord came down upon Mount Sinai, on the top of the mount: and the Lord called Moses up to the top of the mount; and Moses went up" (vs. 20).

Moses had gone only part way up the mount. It wasn't until God called to him to approach the top, to enter the cloud and appear before the very presence of God Himself that Moses was able to move forward.

You see, man in his own power cannot enter the presence of God. God must let him come in. Man needs help. He needs redemption. He cannot enter heaven in his own strength or power. No matter how good a man may be, he needs God's help. God must open the door. God must open the way.

Moses went inside the cloud, "and the sight of the glory of the Lord was like devouring fire on the top of the mount in the eyes of the children of Israel." Moses was in the cloud, in the very presence of God for "forty days and forty nights" (Exodus 24:16-18).

To Flesh and Blood

It amazes me that God chose to give His sacred message to a mortal born of woman. It wasn't to angels the holy words were given. It wasn't to any heavenly host, or to the stars or any other creature. God's message of love, guidance, and redemption was given to man. "What is man, that thou art mindful of him? For thou has made him a little lower than the angels, and has crowned him with glory and honor" (Psalm 8:5,6). The rabbinic sages say that God shrouded Moses with the cloud so that Satan could not find him. In other words, as God was giving Moses His sacred Words to record, God was protecting him from the wrath of the evil one.

I marvel that God would give His message to man. God's name is to be honored (Psalm 8:9), and yet, God has magnified His word above his very name (Psalm 138:2)...and then gives it to man. "And God spake all these words..." (Exodus 20:1).

Amazing!

Shavuot

The Jews commemorate this encounter with God. The holiday is called *Shavuot.* It is celebrated in May or June, 50 days after the Passover. It is one of the seven feasts described in Leviticus 23. It became known as the day Moses received the Law from Mount Sinai. It is a time that marks Israel's spiritual journey.

This holiday is no small event as Jewish people remember the time God met with a man and gave him a message. The message is found in the first five books of the Bible called the Torah or Pentateuch. These are the books of Moses. He wrote down what God said to him. He wrote down the words that God wanted the people to know.

Pentecost

Pentecost is the Greek of the Hebrew Shavuot. It is the same holiday. However, Christians celebrate Pentecost remembering that 10 days after Messiah's ascension the Holy Spirit came in His fullness and the Church was born (Acts 2) and thousands came to believe in Jesus.

Jesus rose from the dead on the third day and appeared before many (1 Corinthians 15). "For the third day the Lord will come down in the sight of all the people upon Mount Sinai" (Exodus 19:11). When Jesus died on the cross the curtain in the temple that separated the people from the Holy of Holies was torn in two. This opened the entrance to the place where the cloud, the Shekinah, the Glory or presence of God appeared.

On this day common bread was eaten. Not the special bread of the other holidays. The common man could easily participate in the celebration. When the curtain was torn and the place was opened up it was exposed to all who would pass by the Temple. The main doors were opened and everyone could see directly into the most sacred place of all.

Pentecost is a celebration of the birth of the church. It commemorates the fact that all believers are indwelt by the Holy Spirit. Because they are indwelt by the Holy Spirit they have access to God directly. They can enter His presence through relationship and faith. The common man, not only a High Priest, can approach God through His Word and Spirit. The curtain was torn, the veil removed, and all who come through the cross and believe can enter a personal relationship with God in Christ.

The Christian Meaning

1. <u>Respect the Holy</u>
   God told Moses to take off his shoes for he was standing on holy ground (Exodus 3:5). In a world where little reverence is expressed for things of God, we are reminded in this account, to pause and value that which is from the Holy One.

   On the south side of the Temple we find that the steps leading up to this sacred place are designed in a certain way. You have one wide step and then on narrow step. You must pause and pay attention while you ascend. If not, you may stumble climbing the steps. That was the idea. To pause, and reflect; to realize, that where you were ascending was a holy place that needed respect and reverence.

The Bible, baptism, communion, preaching and teaching of the Scripture, the place where God's people meet are to name a few things holy that need our respect and reverence.

2. Worship the Holy One

When you bring forth the people…you shall worship God… (Exodus 3:12). The Hebrew word *"abad"* translated "serve" can also be rendered "worship" or "enslaved". Isn't it interesting that God would say something like this, "When you free my people from enslavement in Egypt, I want them to be enslaved to me. Then, they will be truly free." True worship is submission to God. "I and the lad will go yonder and worship" (Genesis 22:5).

To be free from your own control, your own desires, your own plan, your own way and letting God have His way in your life is the only way to be truly free.

3. Journey Alone

Each one of us must seek God. You alone must come to terms with God. Moses was in the desert when he found God, or, actually, when God approached Moses. Just as Jesus approached and found the disciples and asked them to follow, so it is that God may approach you. However, you alone must respond to Him. Either you believe, or you deny. But you do it alone.

4. God will Comfort

   "We shall be satisfied with the goodness of thy house" (Psalm 65:4). As we journey through life we will have mountain top experiences as well as dark valleys of trial and testing. In all of these we are reminded that God will comfort. As Moses "went up to God" God called to him and gave Moses His precious Word. The follower of God will come to know the profound comfort of Scripture. The Holy Spirit takes these ancient words and brings healing to the soul. "Let my soul live, and it shall praise thee" (Psalm 119:175). Why does my soul live? "Thy word hath quickened me" (Psalm 119:50). In other words, God's Word brings life.

5. To Man God's Word was Given

   It was to Moses the ancient message was given. God entrusted His message to man. To celebrate this magnificent, mysterious moment in time the Jews celebrate Shavuot commemorating the giving of the Law to Moses. They decorate their homes, eat special foods with milk and honey products reminding them of the land of milk and honey.

   Milk and honey are symbols of Torah and learning. In the synagogue the book of Ruth is read during Shavuot. Oftentimes, before reading the Scriptures at home, Jewish families will place a drop of honey on the tongue of each child (even babies). Some will even pour honey on the page of the text and have the child lick the honey off the page. Why? "How sweet are thy words unto my taste! Yea, sweeter than honey to my mouth" (Psalm 119:103). The child associates the learning of Scripture as something sweet.

6. To Man God's Spirit was Given

Christians call Shavuot *"Pentecost"*. There were thunders and lightnings, a thick cloud and a sound of a trumpet (shofar) when Moses ascended the mountain. Pentecost was also a day marked by unique events. "A sound from heaven as of a rushing mighty wind", "There appeared cloven tongues like as of fire". (Acts 2:2,3).

Just like the eerie sound of the trumpet on Mount Sinai, the wind blew on Mount Zion. And, just like the thunders and lightnings appeared on Mount Sinai, the cloven fire appeared on Mount Zion. On this day the followers of Moses received the Law on Mount Sinai. On this day, 1500 years later, the followers of Jesus the Messiah received the Holy Spirit and the birth of the Church on Mount Zion.

The Shofar

A side note here: The first reference of the Shofar (ram's horn) in Scripture is found when Moses went up to God. The shofar was also used to announce the beginning of the Shabbat. Joshua used the shofar to bring the walls down. All throughout the Tanakh (Old Testament) you will find references to the shofar. Some say that it was Abraham who blew the shofar for the first time to worship God in providing the ram in Genesis 22.

It is interested to note that the blowing of the shofar is associated with the return of Messiah and the rapture of the Church (Matthew 24:31; 1Corinthians 15:52; 1 Thessalonians 4:16). The Jewish Tanakh ends with 2 Chronicles with a reference of "going up". The B'rit Hadashah (New Covenant; New Testament) ends with "Come up hither" & "even so come Lord Jesus" (Revelation 4:1; 22:20). Moses went up – the Church will go up.

Begin Your Ascent

God has opened the way for salvation through His son Jesus. The gift of salvation has been paid for on the cross. Therefore, eternal life is given to all who believe in Jesus as the Son of God, who is God Himself. However, the journey of sanctification, or spiritual growth and maturity is a difficult journey. It is, as it were, a journey up the mountain. Nevertheless, each Christian must decide to ascend. God will not force you to climb. If you begin to climb, the cost will be great and the path difficult.

God will be with you each step of the way. He will call out to you through His Word and Spirit. He will protect you from the evil one. If you decide to climb, you will never be the same. Like Moses, it will take courage, it will take commitment, it will take faith, and you must go alone. But it will be worth it!

Begin your ascent now and trust God.

"Fear not: for I have redeemed thee, I have called thee by thy name; thou art mine. When thou passest through the waters, I will be

with thee; and through the rivers, they shall not overflow thee: when thou walkest through the fire, thou shalt not be burned; neither shall the flame kindle upon thee, for I am the Lord thy God the Holy One of Israel, thy Savior" (Isaiah 43:1-3)